IT IS ALL EQUALLY FRAGILE

ALISON MALEE

THOUGHT CATALOG Books

THOUGHTCATALOG.COM

THOUGHT
CATALOG
Books

Copyright © 2024 Alison Malee.

All rights reserved. No part of this book may be reproduced or transmitted in any form or any means, electronic or mechanical, without prior written consent and permission from Thought Catalog.

Published by Thought Catalog Books, an imprint of Thought Catalog, a digital magazine owned and operated by The Thought & Expression Co. Inc., an independent media organization founded in 2010 and based in the United States of America. For stocking inquiries, contact stockists@shopcatalog.com.

Produced by Chris Lavergne and Noelle Beams
Designed and illustrated by KJ Parish
Circulation management by Isidoros Karamitopoulos

thoughtcatalog.com | shopcatalog.com

First Edition, Limited Edition Pressing
Printed in the United States of America

ISBN 978-1-949759-80-8

contents

I
9

II
41

III
73

IV
107

*I have loved and been loved,
and it is all equally fragile.*

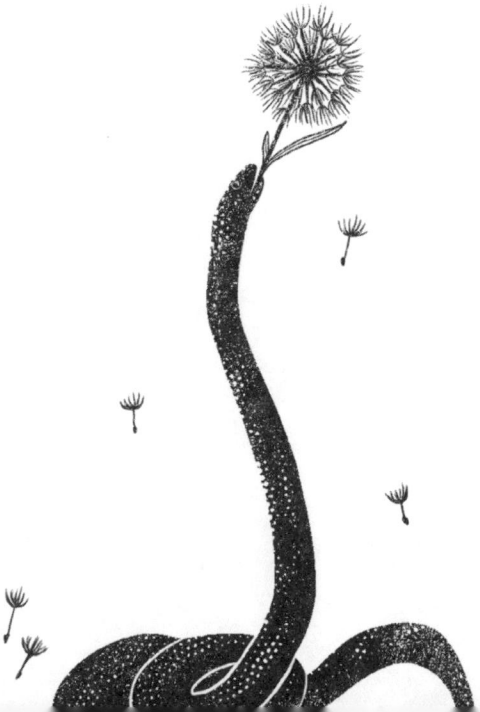

A collection of ordinary, fragile moments.

I

If I am to tell a story, let it be an honest one.
Let it pour from me freely and without hesitation.
Let it be, amongst other things, a lighthouse.

GASOLINE, REGULAR

Right when I believed myself invincible,
I fell in love. Only diesel at the gas station,
green pumps for miles. Sneakers at a dance club.
Heels on the couch, shoulders shimmying. Never
a dull knife, never a sharp knife, never a knife at all.
Everything cut with scissors. Everything dug
up with feet. Symphonies of layered bass drums.
Snares welcome. In December, drawer after drawer
of tank tops. In July, thick wool. Cashmere. Flannel.
Ask me of current events, or take this flower
from my garden, they are the same. Love
leaks from me. I am flammable now, by definition.

I KEEP THIS VISION

For a time after my daughter's birthday, we raised
caterpillars from a clear, plastic jar. We observed,
as good scientists do. In between coffee and
schedules, it's own form of spiritual ritual.

Their squirming bodies. Their cocoons
shivering with movement. Muddled and sticky
in their habitat, base insects scrounging about
as base insects do.

Then, one day, our home was filled with the sound of unrest,
butterflies emerging all at once, orange, red, spotted,
pulsing with new need.

That night, my daughter, all of seven years,
held the cage open with quivering, small hands,
shuffling from foot to foot as anticipation held her close.

The sky had gone gray and unremarkable,
and yet we waited for each one
to discover a path to the top and take flight.

I keep this vision; her eyes fixed on a pair of velvet wings.
An artist, or a mother's tender pleasure
growing in the corners—so insistent that miracles exist
it bubbled up from her chest and spilled over.

The months change,
and the seasons shift,

and the days start to grow
into darkness early—

making the nights
their own grasping eternities.

THIS I KNOW ABOUT LOSS

A small bird has come to tap hesitantly
at my window and the earth is spinning.

My hand floats up, a marionette, to press
the fresh fruit of my palm to the glass as an offering.

Hello, my own heart made anew, hope
a poem still churning. This little silhouette

of tucked-in wings is one I am learning
to recognize. Then, I am slipping my shoes

off, blinking as I place hardened heels
into high stirrups. A long moment passes

without sound. The technician pats my arm
with a rubber hand, *'go home and focus*

on your children,' she smiles. Hollow as any
forgotten log, I do. Grief gnaws with an aching

persistence. The body reciprocates. In weathered
pages of medical journals, this is the unexplained;

how to grieve a love never held. A wilting slant
of light. For a time, every morning, it begins again—

the prayer, the window, the slow sinking pit
in the gut. If I am being honest, too many days

sit between now and then. I still search for (you)r
new, downy feathers.

WHEN THE LAST WINTER COAT HAS BEEN PUT AWAY

Neither of us remember to grab the mail.
I shave my legs for the first time in months.

Our daughters catch you whistling a flighty tune
and giggle as you chase them back out into the yard.

Spring cradles us like a fresh babe.
We are helpless to the allure of freckles, heat, play.

On the worn wood of a weathered outdoor table,
there is a tray heavy with tomatoes, and a glass

salt shaker standing in the puddled runoff.
Between teeth caught chewing and a bout of

breathy laughter, I mash red and seeds.
Sure, I can tell you a handful of silver linings

about winter, but at some point, the cold withers
all living things. Give me sunburn. Give me long,

slow hours. Give me the sound of a full house
rippling along an evening breeze.

A POINT OF VIEW

What do you see through the window?
A series of skyscrapers? The bottom of an ocean?

The crack in your teeth becoming
a garden of dried and hung bouquets.

The soft way a wound closes over.
Strangers who may one day kiss you on the mouth.

A life that could have been yours.
Small-town nowhere. Robin's egg eyes.

We see what we want to see
from the windows we choose to sit in front of.

I see flowers on the table. I see spring sprouting
from the veins of everyone I have ever met.

LEARNING INTO MYSELF

The mailman tucks today's newspaper
under the front door, and I haven't made any headlines.

A man marries a woman. A woman marries a woman.
Someone rescues a small dog from a well.

Does the power of social media eclipse
traditional media? Will we go back to the moon?

I tell you, I burnt both of my heels as I walked
across the ocean, but no one reported on it.

I learned my name at twenty-four, left my body
in a bed somewhere and climbed into the day

with renewed purpose. There is not a single
judge or jury but my memories.

I imagined recognition would keep the coil
of abandonment from springing.

But it turns out today's newspaper is an emptying
of stories, and none of them are mine. Mine is

waiting; cotton threaded through the tip of a needle.
Pressed wine stirring in the dark of a cellar.

The tart flesh of anchored fruit broiled sweet,
caramelized in the sun; a poem in the mouth.

SOUR ORANGE JUICE AND A STIFF-BACKED CHAIR

Alison is playing on the radio at the cafe that I have sat myself in all morning.

If I believed in coincidences, I would call this one.
It doesn't need to be divine to be significant.

A man in a black hat nearby reclines with his own coffee in a thermos. An elderly couple who shared a breakfast pastry but each ordered a large coffee for themselves stare out a muggy window.

There are three women in the corner who have been here as long as I have been, deep in conversation with their heads bent towards each other.

Some days I fear I'll never learn anything more, that all the rumbling of curiosity will vanish, a grinning cat in the wind.

Some days I fear I've learned all there is to know, and I wonder what my work will look like then. How will I ponder over anything long enough to write about it?

But when I sit again in front of the paper, it is still a list of questions that appears.

As if someone in another seat, looking at another group of strangers, hears her name playing softly over crackling speakers too and wonders if anyone will notice if she sings along.

THE ART OF AGING POORLY

The news anchor is laughing
with his co-host about the heat.

He says, *We gotta find joy in the smallest things
these days, don't we, Sandy?*

Look, Brad, I mumble,
there isn't art on the inside of everything.

Sometimes a song is only a song.
Sometimes it is hot, and August moans
with endless heat, leaves the air wet
and tangible as it snakes across the city.

If the radio still played music like it used to,
it would play something classic,
a singular guitar solo
that spanned the whole three minutes,

And we would laugh about how badly
we needed ice cream on a day like this.

But instead, the kids request snacks
from the back seat of the car,
and I sing softly, rattling off
the grocery list in my head.

Brad returns with the latest scoop
on some celebrity, and Sandy lets him.

We pull into our neighborhood
 just as a group of teenagers
flood outside from a nearby house, all tank tops and sweat.
Someone, everyone, is laughing
as they dart and weave
through the yard, the distinct sound
of flip flops echoing after them.

Without blinking, I roll up the window.

AFTER YEARS OF MARRIAGE

We exist quietly. Only you, rubbing
the soft spot behind my ear the way
solitude used to, constant and confident.

UNALTERED GRIEF

Just now, my mother calls to tell me
that from her window, clouds hover

in a straight line like a shelf across
the Colorado mountains.

She wants to know what I can see,
and I open my mouth to tell her

that from here, the dust settles
over everything like my brother's ashes.

It is dark, the dark you have to
wade through slowly, palms flat.

Instead, I tell her there is a bird mid-flight;
neck elongated, brows furrowed

like it is contemplating the journey,
the directions, the destination, the sky.

When I hang up the call, I spread out
my small, pink, human arms as far as they will go.

ADULTHOOD

Coffee in hand,
book in my lap,

a little less money
than the day before.

I chase the sun
with my eyes,

watch shadows flicker
like black and white

photographs
caught in the wind.

When the phone rings,
it isn't good news,

and the windows
rattle with it.

The coffee splatters.
The book closes.

The money dissolves
like sugar in hot, hot water;

as if it never held
weight to begin with.

Sometimes
I have not seen joy for weeks,
but I know it will come.

DEFINITIONS

Love is the ripening of fruit,
not the withering.

Is a mouth full
of good, learned words.

Good sentences, good poetry.
Good, inquisitive poetry.

Is the arc of the moon.
The flint of a matchstick.

The grace of a sloping wing.
Is laughter trickling past caution

and barreling into salvation.

HEART'S DESIRE

What I desire
        is to swell like
                an ocean in the night.
      A fitful process, then,
a slow, lingering retreat
               as waves do,
     before swallowing
  back up
            the land left behind.
  Only, in the end,
I remember your faces
            and I stay.

JONAH OR ADAM OR STEVE

So the whale swallowed someone whole.
Unassuming man down. Scientifically speaking,
this is not a revelation. Who among us cares
to punish hunger? What's more, any wicked,
weeping woman could unclench the jaw
just as well. Pop tendons for the silken
swallow of brine and bone—every bit
as animal. A full moon curse (or) another
Wednesday afternoon. Point us to the enemy.
Grease the hinges. There is room in the gut.

A MOTHER

Blue wasn't always
the color of the ocean.

Thirty years ago, blue
belonged only to a set

of eyes that startled

when a baby
was thrust into the world.

Before the world burst

into bright,
shimmering blue—

there was only a
colorless ocean.

THANKSGIVING, AGE THREE

Palm flat in the center
of your chipped porcelain plate,

you lick all of the cranberry
from your hand in between
spurts of warbled giggles.

This is how you give thanks,
bless the meal, say grace.

For today, I celebrate with you
and your sticky fingers.

For as long as you are this little,
I will smile at all of the syrup
dripping down your chin.

AFTER WANDERING INTO THE YARD

The deer and I hold eye contact
for two full, slow-breathing

minutes before I say hello.
He tilts his head and blinks

once, twice. I sit down slowly,
hunched in the grass to shrink myself

more prey than predator,
suddenly overcome by my own

heartbeat; that old, thrumming
loneliness. The deer turns,

walks back towards the trees,
growing smaller as he travels

away, away, out of view. And
the day grows ordinary.

THAT LIVES

There is, of course, the self
that lived before responsibility

made dreams feel small and benign,
little cells in a dish waiting

to grow into organisms of their own.
Before morning routines, before

insistent calculations. Gas prices,
inflation, appointments, *etcetera*,

etcetera. I may wander back
to an old self one day, and

discover it is not me anymore.
Not the same hands, certainly.

Not better or broken. No, the body
is simply always reinventing itself.

Every little thing can be
considered a mercy
the universe grants us.

ATTEMPTING FAITH, AGE 29

You say your prayers that it is
this life you have been woven into.

AN EARLY LOSS, OR
THERE IS A SEASON FOR EVERYTHING

In the bathroom, I am watching
shadows pull and stretch like muscle;

a season I was not prepared for
already blooming across the tissue.

Even if the body is only doing
what the body needs to do, I beg it not to.

My tongue hanging out like a dog in heat,
all manner of promises at the end of it—

lapping up any hint of a miracle.
The loudest and quietest my grief has ever been.

That's when the dream rose up in me,
a hand shaking its fist into the wind.

Please, do not make me
introduce myself to emptiness.

Hope is simple; despite
the overwhelming impossibility.

And I, already a mother.

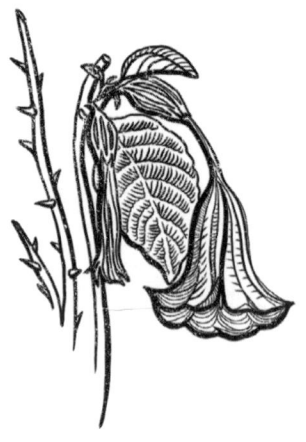

COMING BACK

The cold makes us reach in the back
of the closet for warm jackets.

When we find them, we carry
our makeshift lunches out to the deck.

Fresh air beckons, but the patio furniture
is already stored for the winter.

It is no matter; when the call sounds, we listen,
and we sit on the crumbling steps instead.

Your braids bounce, my hair flies,
and in time to the rhythm of our chewing
we swing our feet, bump our shoulders.

Growing up is hard on the imagination.
But we laugh real laughter, the truest kind.

Like we are both so very young,
like motherhood has not aged me.

And my god, look at the sun.
It keeps coming back.

II

OCCURRENCES

On a field trip, the kids find
a frog in the grass. A little girl

presses it so tightly into her
palm all of the chaperones gasp.

A fat-bellied bee lands on the edge
of my teacup, and when he leaves,

I drink it anyway. Monday afternoon
rain hits the house like stomping

boots. In Connecticut, the highway
is lined only with trees. We watch

them go by for miles. An entire bag
of grapes waits to be eaten in the

freezer, and I tell no one. At a school
function, I am a two-way mirror.

The blade of the chainsaw cuts
into the trunks of all the trees

in our yard, one after the other.
A family of stray cats makes

a home of the hollow space beneath
our front steps, and on the doorbell

camera, we hear them singing to each other.
You loved me, once, I am sure of it.

HAND OVER

When my friend asks me to sign
her marriage certificate,

I panic about the permanence of love.
At the reception, she leans her forehead

on her husband's chest as they sway,
sealing them close like the peel

of a clementine and the tender flesh
beneath, no space between them.

And I think of you. Imperfect
and honest and mine. Does love give us

something, a benevolent god, or
are we always the willing sacrifice

at the altar? Say there

is no guarantee. Hand over a love
that has been swollen and infatuated,

puckered and sour, limp and corrupt.
Give her a love like ours, that sees

a window and knows light survives
the dark-drunk lure of shadows—

isn't afraid to let you guess at the thing,
even when it knows the answer.

ALRIGHT

Our bodies,
especially
our bodies,

are meant
for compassion.

Meant to hold
it tightly.

Meant to press
it to our chest
like a new babe—

rocking gingerly,
murmuring,

thank you,
I love you too,

it's all going
to be alright.

UNANNOUNCED

And wildly,
I find laughter

like
hot breath,

mouth to mouth,

amen amen

ricocheting
through my chest.

TAKE THESE FOR THE EVENING

A hummingbird's heart can beat 1,000 beats per minute
and I must be one of them. Sugar high frenzy, flitting

from one branch to the next, dancing light of distended sun.
Lover, stranger, tender lips. A home for the evening.

We kissed just once. Outside of the grocery store,
mouth to mouth. In his dim apartment, water boiled.

Onions shed skin across a cutting board, smug
in their sensuality. Butter, tomatoes, garlic.

Simmering pan. Wine-drunk, frenetic, buzzing
at our ability to create something whole from

separate somethings. Here, take these. A tender
molding of my mouth. In French this is how we say

spaghetti, friend, dawn. Approaching, regardless.

TIME IS A MEDIATOR

Today, the stains in the carpet
make the tears run.

The water cup knocked over
makes the tears run.

The burnt almonds on the stove
make the tears run, too.

Forgive me, this living with you
and then living without you

still feels experimental.
Today, loss says, *'nothing is as it was,'*

and I nod along. What if we meet
again, when we each have less

to carry? We can pretend
we have not missed a thing.

A TRIP INTO NEW JERSEY

A state away from home, I barter for two cast
iron pots from a woman who lives on a flat acre

with no trespassing signs. When I eye the cracked paint,
white bubbling up and out, she huffs

smoked wind chimes. 'People have
to love old things for their flaws,' and sure,

age is skin we wear only briefly. Forget youth.
Anything can be caught beautiful in its prime.

Praise the rust, the wrinkle, the sunspot.
Praise the crooked spine, the whisker, the graying.

Praise the decay, the moss-covered
sweat of forest floor, the wayward teeth.

Something about greed trying to tame.
What good is anything not made entirely by chance?

STANDING AT THE EDGE

Consider: it is fear that widens
the gap between trust
and the willingness to jump.

LOOSEN MY GRIP

Everything I have ever held
has fingerprints.

I STILL DO NOT KNOW
MUCH ABOUT ANYTHING

What is a cartwheel, and how do you trust
momentum to push you over? By what age

should a portfolio no longer relate to art class,
and have more to do with money? Better yet,

by what age does money begin to lose its grip?
Does anyone, anywhere, know the key to creating

balance? When do you let go of friendships
that do not serve you? How long would it take

to start over somewhere new? If time is a balm,
what is the minimum amount before the white

cast settles into skin? Does grief ever learn to
leave well enough alone? What happens if,

relentlessly, you pick at the scab? Because
believe me, my fingers itch.

THE CHOICE

A flush of wings and mother bird nestles in
over her matted nest on the outer rim of sloped roof.

Silent but for the push and pull of lungs,
I watch from the stoop of our porch as

her eyes close, chest humming as she settles.
Tender as any hallelujah.

Does worry startle her in the night, too? Does she wake
breathless, feathers at attention, rings like ripe plums

pressed beneath her eyes as she keeps watch?

We are all choosing to live—choosing to live!—
and praying it will be a choice that is honored.

When we wake, and fear is only the spilled cereal,
the unbrushed hair, the minutes on the clock,

when all will be well; when we are not carrying
around these dead, unavoidable things.

INTERNAL NAVIGATION

I hear a hiss and call it rain. At the next stop,
blame the wind. But in the garage the sound

is insistent, unraveling what little peace I scraped
together. Turns out, a fat, metal screw lodged itself

into my tire somewhere between home and
school drop off, and the mechanic wants to know

if my husband or father will be coming by to help.
When he refers to me as little lady, I even manage to

twitch the corner of my mouth upward in the name of
decorum. He repairs the feathered rubber. I ask

the standard questions. My shoulders become
well acquainted with my earlobes. Later, when

the blank page seeks retribution, the only words
that come to mind are ones a good *little lady*

would never say. I am without guilt. For some time
now, I have planned to be bothered by no one

and nothing. Purposefully unchecked. That is
the real story. How gloriously justified it is

to want nothing more than to fall asleep
all alone, absolutely feral. Decorum be damned.

After all of this,
being afraid
is a house in which
we have shattered
all of the windows.

ON BECOMING A WRITER

Right there in the heart
of the page, the poet spies a
newborn rabbit quivering.
We all arrive here eventually,
hunkered down in the field,
stroking fur. One day, you,
yourself, will be bent in the same
odd way, almost doubled in half,
murmuring into downy ears.

The angle won't even concern you.
Neither will the damp grass, or
the questioning eyes of the neighbors.
Imagine, by then, it will have become
second nature, this little bit of
discomfort required for the chance
to uncover what, exactly, the poem
is trying to tell you.

SEARCHING FOR THE VILLAGE

We have nowhere to store our loneliness,
and so the world becomes a lover.

WHAT GOOD WOULD IT DO TO GIVE UP NOW?

When there is earth,
scrappy and stomped on

that, without shame,
continues to push

forth new work
in the lilac light

of dawn, even with
the critics in her ear,

even with the sun
a pointed finger.

SO SURE

From the confines of her car seat,
my toddler wails. She would like

the music louder, louder, please
and I am human, too.

We screech-sing until our throats hurt
and the song swells between us

on an empty, darkening road.
When it is bass and voices, only,

I look up, so sure heaven can hear us.

Finally, someone might answer
my wretched, wretched prayers.

FEELS LIKE HOME

If I wanted the earth to open up

    and swallow me,

I could conjure a thousand different variations,
    but not today.

Today your chest is warm.
    The earth feels like home.

    To stay does not have to mean

    anything more
        than delight
    in the small ways the universe

says grace, and amen,
        for its own offerings.

    How this praise,
        sometimes and quietly,
    overcomes

the gravity of living.

MADE SOLID BY BELIEF

In a dream, my husband and I buy a home that our friends and family *just know* is haunted.
We plan to clean the pool and hang white linen curtains in the living room.

The day we move in, I spend the morning swinging open every kitchen cabinet, and when I reach the one above the stove, stock-piled baking supplies fall to the ground. Sprinkles, metal cookie cutters, plastic piping bags.

And yes, in a different dream, the car fills with water, and we blow from the seats through the windows, grasping at branches of passing trees, leaves between our fingers.
With water in my throat, I call your name.

Ghosts are only made solid by belief.

—

Our neighbors are moving down south and bring our children old soccer balls. Their son, tall in his gym shorts, bends all the way down to speak tenderly to my daughters.

Then he tells me, '*My parents are tired of the winters here.*'
I own more coats than desire to stay, too.

Save for the mail lady, Diane, who signs for my packages when I cannot meet her at the mailbox. Her voice carries the soft gravel of knowing things. I remind myself, again, to ask her when her birthday is.

—

I am almost thirty. Did I mention, as we speak, there is something unimaginably wonderful happening somewhere to someone? So it goes without saying that there is sorrow happening somewhere, too.

—

My sister doesn't call when she finds out about the baby. Only sends a message. Not the written kind in a bottle, the kind that includes her husband and my husband and isn't really addressed to me at all.

—

But then, love is a ghost. We make it solid. We hang white linen curtains in its living room. We ask strangers to help us do everyday things, like pick up packages, bring us old things they do not need any longer, leave behind baking supplies we may keep. We buy haunted places with all of our savings and pray for good outcomes. Pray for something unimaginably wonderful.

—

At the pool, my daughter plays marco polo with the other children even though she does not know how to swim. She yells '*Marco,*' and the children all dive to the center of the pool, gargling salt as they giggle, scream back, '*Polo!*'

All of her pruning little fingers squeeze along the edge of the concrete sides as she makes her way around the perimeter. With water in her throat, she calls their names and laughs.

TO MOST HUMAN EYES

The fly with the molten,
bulging orange peel eyes

sees everything as if reflected
through a kaleidoscope.

How must he see me?
A thousand versions of the same

face, which, to most human eyes,
must look the same.

ANY LEARNED FEAR CAN BE UNLEARNED

Three generations
of women in my family
have disbanded

at the sight of
scales and flicking
tongue.

What is ever what
we mean it to be
when we find it
out of habit?

After a quarter
of a century,
I still swallow
the residual shudder.

A snake in the grass
is a creature
surviving the
same sharp world.

BRIGHT STARS

We've made it to the end of another year
and my father holds my hand only briefly.

He says, *'Memories, huh?'* as the crowd shuffles
out from the theater in unison, a sea of starlings.

The language of firsts has swelled in him,
rampant, and I know he can't explain it.

Because who can? Every once in a while
the passage of time is so startling

it leaps, and yearns, lifts without fanfare.

Just yesterday, I laughed shyly with a sweet,
new boy for the very first time.

Today, I woke up beside a man who will
kill the spiders if I ask him to,

but knows me enough to capture and release
all eight black, furled limbs outside.

Memories, huh?

Of course, I will remember the bright, hurling stars
folding themselves gently into the night sky.

FOR ONLY

Today is held together
by the same worry as yesterday.

I wash the dishes and worry
nestles itself into the foam.

I fold bath towels and crumpled
pajamas as worry sinks into

the creases. I hum a song so
endless my teeth begin to rattle.

All the while, worry floats
ahead and behind me,

muttering on and on. Just look
at all of these things we carry

without even questioning.
How do I make room for

faith only, for love only—
only for forgiveness.

I ADMIT,
IT IS COMPLICATED

But love can be
as simple as grabbing
their packages from the
porch before it rains.

I keep thinking, loss is a well.
There is bound to be a hand,

a rope, a light over hushed water.
So here I am, floating. A good study

in patience, practicing my breathing.

UNFETTERED

Like that,
the funeral
was over.

Outside of my
brother's old
stomping grounds,

my family swayed
and hollered,
dipped and shimmied.

Unfettered by foolishness,
or temporarily,
the stark brutality
of new grief.

Together
until our bodies
commanded us
motionless.

III

IVORY

We carried with us the secret of each other.
The sweat of mid-afternoon heat

and tangle, a damp warmth in our back pockets.
We were young and the act of choosing

each other still felt scandalous. Then, a heaving,
gorged breath escaped you, and no one else

was there to witness this unceremonious death.

A name careened from your tongue, hit the air
with a thump. Almost parasitic in the way

it sucked the sun back into the clouds—
and was not mine. It hung low in the air,

hovering as fruit flies do, low as drooping berries
flop cheeked animals chew apart at the bottom

of the vine. Even if I begged for you to stuff
the name back, it was there now demanding attention.

So the image formed. My mouth nettled and bleeding.
You said you didn't *need* but you *wanted*,

until it was insatiable. What is it to be a man?
To always hunger? This is often how

I think of you now; hunched low to the flat
bed of earth, grunting, beating your chest.

An ivory-stained bone
ground between your teeth.

KEEP YOU SAFE

The first time alone in a city and the sprawling
underbelly swells, an unhinged orchestra. Decay

like violin strings. Subway platforms another home
for haggard dreamers, the stench of cramped desire

a possessive smog, the last thrum of a crescendo.
Now, you flatten yourself to peeling sub-level walls,

unshaken by the thrash of crowd. The sweltering press
of other skin, the beat of drums, approaching next stops,

drunken cheers. His hand on her knee, and her hand
on his elbow, and his hand on his shoulder.

The person on the phone weeping quietly
in the corner. The man with his legs spread wide,

elbows braced, taking up two seats because he can.
Wear that smile that says *thank you, of course,*

after you, no please, don't even worry about it,
but don't touch me, don't mess with me, don't

you even dare. Evolution of alone. Shoulders back,
chin high, screen unlocked in case of emergency.

UNRULY

God calls
to me mostly
as slow breath
in through the nose,
new, sheepish bud,
small song of
crickets in the grass,
train grinding onto
the track early,
your shadow form
rising off of the edge
of the bed
without complaint,
as you wake
for a job that does
not feed you,
in the unruly
morning hours.

MARVELED

*Humans will always be curious
to the point of desperation,*

you murmur from your propped-
up place above my shoulder.
It seems as logical
an explanation as any.

Days later, our daughter
loses a front tooth—
yanks it clean out and wipes
the blood off on her pajamas.

One hand high in the air, clutching
her prized possession, the other
on her hip. She proclaims that anyone,
anywhere, can feel this
kind of joy if they want to,
and your logic wobbles.

I have marveled at a thing,
not known how to hold it.
And lost in my pleasure,
not needed a proper
explanation either.

Joy—the kind that is
insistent, never ushers in
desperation to make a point.

It finds the thread
of intrigue and pulls.

HELP IS OFFERED AND I

Unlock the door,
make it a habit.

SHIFTS AND LEANS

What sustains us but the body, even when the body is swept under the curtain of exhaustion? Even when thoughts crowd in close as if seeking warmth, trampling each other for room. Even when the body is left unattended, not given permission to wither, but withering anyway. Even when the universe pauses, you, at the coffee shop with your three children, unable to claw the sleep from your cheekbones. And the young girl, the one in her wide-legged jeans and tight boots, with her frozen drink and cute dessert, calls to you to let you know that "*Ma'am, your drink is here*" and *ma'am* guts you in a way nothing prepared you for, the weight of age gripping your shoulders like skeleton fingers.

Even when you miss sixteen and eighteen and twenty-one, when you miss eating a ball of cake on a stick in the chatter of a cafe, the body shifts and leans and embraces, and even with the ache of creaking bones, holds you upright, is firm in its existence, understands that when the kids go to bed, you may curse it, cherish it, thank it, may howl at the moon for a passing moment, may sit in the dark and stew, face lit up by a dim screen, may order a pair of jeans, completely unrelated to anything else, with slightly wider hems.

FORGET THE BOOK

At book club we talk about the orbital—
our spouses, children, careers. We circle, birds
of prey with small talk as talons.

Do not touch. Eat light snacks on paper
plates, small bites only. Avoid our own demons.

Print the questions provided by the publisher.
Read another suburban murder mystery.

Laugh about the waif of a protagonist,
her disdain for society and her crumbling

marriage. *One of them will snap, inevitably,*
we say, *anyone's guess*. Both driven mad,

threadbare and lonely. But look at us, not
tethered to ourselves or each other in any way.

When I get home, I rattle my husband
with my rage. *Forget the book*, I cry—

how does it feel when the last lamp is turned
off at night? Have you ever let yourself

dream past where you are now? Does anything
scare you, deep down in your bones? Do you worry

that you are living a good life? Are you writing
the kind of story that fulfills you? Are you brave
enough to start over?

Next month, I bring the chips and salsa.

THE EVIDENCE OF SUBURBIA

makes itself known at the dinner table.
The grain of old pine grazed with small fingers,
wrinkled fingers, grown up and growing older fingers.
Heat spills up and out from the oven,
from the scrunched-in bodies gathered; spooled
like honey across bread. It isn't as if we haven't
seen the news. It isn't as if we haven't swiped
through the images, held the gravity. In the kitchen,
a timer summons and steam rises from something
requiring more than one set of hands. There is
a sense of urgency. Still, feet shuffle;
a quick stretch before beginning.

BACK AS SAPLINGS

in the next life. All of a sudden, weightless
and infinite as all new things. Both to recognize

that to expand, there must be rain, and to seize
what it is to keep ourselves warm in the dark.

THE UNIVERSE IS TEEMING WITH EYELASHES

Black. Espresso. Soft brown.
Auburn. Pale yellow. Ivory.

Forget the bones, ancient ritual, sun
and moon aligned, whisper of sea.

There is the slight curve of a black downy
eye feather on a cheek, on a fingertip,
on the bulb of a nose,

waiting patiently for the glory of wind
to blow it skywards. And when it does,

God swallows the wish
and we become the dream.

AFTER THE BABY

On Thursday, he returns from the store
with two cartons of ice cream.

Blueberry crumble and hot fudge sundae.
My face screws up terribly, half moons like

crushed berries beneath heavy eyes,
exhaustion rewriting reality.

Unwilling to accept a kindness that
does not fit my own imagined, angry narrative.

He doesn't flinch. Hands me a silver,
long-handled spoon from the drawer.

Look around. There is enough evidence
for anyone to find. Evolution is brutal.

We rub each other's wounds
like crickets in the night, healing what we can.

SOCIAL MEDIA BREAK

I keep saying I am going to look up
at that big roof of sky more. Bless

the immediacy of conversation. Sneak out
into tall, damp grass in the middle

of an afternoon. Keep my heart cracked
wide as the running mouth of a river.

Be the river, wild with everything,
awash with blue. Worship the glass prism

wings of dragonflies. Find out if my parents'
eyes still crinkle with the same sincerity. It matters,

that swath of sun leftover from yesterday,
shimmying itself free from the burden of clouds.

It all does. Time is insistent. Still, yesterday,
when the morning groaned awake, I angled

myself in the open screen until I was satisfied. A humble
beggar down on both knees, with no time to spare.

AFTER ALL

I choose love in the morning,
when the sun is meek and simmering.

In the fever of afternoon, as the day beats on,
solid like the thrum of hummingbird wings.

I choose love in the slick eel evening,
as wind tucks us against its quiet underbelly.

When the day fades, and the world
is replaced by its deep, shifting replica.

We are, after all, only specks of light behind our eyes.
Golden, colored brave, in need of tending
until each star stutters out.

AUTUMN

The first tree in our yard to lose her leaves
does so methodically. She wishes

to be witnessed. Her old skin sheds
slowly, a bit more floating to the ground

with each promise of wind, giving way
to bare branches. Limbs bent at the elbow,

so like mine as I wait for you in the evening.
Left alone to my own writhing dance.

She and I are the same. All angles stretching
out towards an invisible tether.

A body being a body being a body.
Wanting as a body does.

MY GRANDMOTHER IS DYING
IN THE MIDDLE OF WINTER

So we load into the car, prepared to take
the endless drive from one corner of the state

to the next. When we pass another long
strip of highway, you take the turn too widely.

Middle America is silent, frosted in mid-winter
as the wheels catch only ice and the car slides—

a broad tree in clear view, road off and away.
Momentum swings us until the sky is dazzling.

We slam against bark and bristle. Jerk. Roll back
towards headlights, yellow lines, oncoming traffic.

Breakfast splashes bright across the dashboard. Static
cranks through the speakers. For a moment, the world

is like the dull ache of an old injury, suspended by
one shuddering heartbeat. After everything we've given,

we cling to the hope that life will spare us.
Give us something back that isn't edged in tragedy.

CINCO DE MAYO AND ALL THE BARS ARE FULL

From one bar to another, our heels slapped
the pavement behind us. Four jaded lovers

with stinging palms. You are visiting America, and me
by extension, for the better part of a week.

We spend half of that time drinking,
the other half trading horror stories.

Tonight, the music is a thrumming Bandaid
in the dark. Our friendship a glass box

in my throat. I refuse to swallow.
You don't dance, have always said you do not

know how, but you smiled like you might love me
as I arched into the pickpocket of bass, arms up.
The only woman I do not have to explain myself to.

And later, shoulder to shoulder, eyes glazed
and breath choppy, we pushed out of a taxi
in front of my apartment.

Stumbled like fresh calves, just as unruly,
and there, on the sidewalk, I stood empty-handed,
bag forgotten in the backseat.

My feet echoed wet splinters down asphalt.
You, a mess of red-gold hair behind me, not going, not gone.

Please come back, I laugh-howled
into the obsidian of stars, *please don't go yet*.

A SERIES OF REQUESTS

Lay me down. Let the space
between our bodies
be something decided.
Let the mask be
secondary for a time.
Open the muscles.
The thrashing sinew.
Spill it all over. Make no move
to clean up the wreckage.
Admit that occasionally
the wreckage is necessary,
confetti strewn on the floor
after a birthday party.
Committing it to memory
each time you walk by
and the whirlwind
of your steps lifts it into the air.
And anyway, look at me.
Insistent beneath you,
a promise hitched in my blood.

UNTO MYSELF, ALWAYS

One summer, another, and another,
endless youth. Pleasure is a girl, a woman,

blazing. I am learning how to wield her
like the wings of a great beast banking

as it reaches the floor of a ravine.

Desire does not aim with precision.
Sometimes, there are casualties.

It is said that we look in the mirror
to inspire loyalty. I swear fealty unto myself,

always. I am blessedly alive. Sweeping
up past the sure death of impact.

TRANSMUTATION

We break against the shore,
little glass bottles churning into sand.

Grieving the bodies we have laid
to rest, the bodies we mourn, the bodies

we have not forgotten. And carefully,
near invisible figments of memory,

exposed, gleaming, rise steadily
from the waves. Bare-chested mist.

Signaling a siren song of farewell
before slipping again below

frothy water. Our own forms,
still restless, amongst the fallen.

THERE IS THE KIND OF POEM

There is the kind of poem that moves you. The kind of poem that looks you in the eye, yes, that smirks at your great confusion. The kind that begs the questions you are too afraid to ask. There is the educational, the informative. The poem that sits in your lap, a fat lazy cat, prodding your knee silently until you feel claws. There is the poem made of tree sap, sticky branch fingers. The poem of underestimation. The poem of a dozen worlds. There is the poem that shimmies. The poem that joins the conga line. The poem that snaps on cue. The poem from the one bedroom of your birthplace. The poem of an eagle, circling. The bad habit poem. There is the knotted poem, the sour stomach poem, the yielding poem. There is the poem in the back of the book, the one the author slid in at the end. A last-ditch poem. The *My editor said I should cut this but I love it too much to part with it* poem. That one I think about often, given as it was, a second chance to go on living.

SETTLING DOWN

Who are we to admit,
after years of weightlessness,
that roots do not actually
threaten anything?

MANY WAYS

There are many ways to carry love:
like a burden, like a gift, like an offering.

FROM JUNE TO SEPTEMBER

After so many months
of sleeping apart, our bones

hum like polarized magnets contracting
and settling. Your arm around

my waist, your leg between
my legs, thighs an antique vise.

Tucked against the patch behind
your ear, my lungs punch out to savor

your innate spice and nutmeg.
Nakedness is effortless. Not once have

I been taught how to forgive
disappointment. Instead, I pry

my thumb from the darkened
bruise of ego. Instead, this smallest, carnal

reunion. Each wordless cry an offered
chord of apology. An intimate,

indecipherable echo.

WHAT IS KEEPING ME ALIVE

A good story coaxed from the throat
of a Monday. The buttery heart

of a poem spread open, knees wide.
Undisturbed sand, shuffle of uniform

playing cards. Supple heat of a lamp
spilling into the evening like glorified syrup.

Buttoned sweaters from childhood. Fast and dirty
swell of a storm. The privilege of being

important to someone. Mostly, my obstinate
heart's merciless stampede. Thundering along, dust

sputtering— dragging me with it.

THE MIRROR

Suppose the body is still surrendering.
Soft as firewood. And briefly, eagerly even,

we fall in love with a sliver of ourselves
as our minds readjust. In the glass,

mouth, belly, breast refracting. Our names
forgettable in this small pocket of thought,

but for once, we call ourselves
the kind of words we deserve to carry.

WHAT IS ANOTHER WORD FOR RAIN?

Goddess of New Beginnings.
Water, obviously. Split clouds.

Spilled miracle of life. *Wet
wet wet*. Ruination or, hear me out,

rebirth. Alchemical transformation.
Heaven unbarred for the hour,

to let the pulse of thirst be a need met.
Quick, or you'll miss it.

ODE TO THE EXPENDABLE

Raise a toast to the tonsils and the baby teeth.
The take-out containers, plastic spoons, sugar packets.

The hair trimmings on the floor of the barber shop.
To jealousy. To self-sacrifice. To enabling bad habits.

To bad habits. To the day my first love got his own
heart broken, and confessed, *If this is how you felt*

when we split, I am so sorry. To embarrassment.
To the unintended consequences of childhood love.

To beets. To cinnamon raisin bread. To coleslaw. To the color
orange for anything beyond a strict three-month
autumnal span.

To insecurity. To unreciprocated pleasure. To capitalism.
To *you hit like a girl*. To abandoned conversations

loitering like little ghosts with unflattering silhouettes.
To conventional. To swallowing our tongues. To stilted
laughter.

To disappearing into roles that do not suit. What if we sit
in the discomfort together, instead, until the knife of it
dissolves?

To this morning, as my daughter cut her hair with blunt-edged
children's scissors. Right to the root, in the space above her
eyebrows.

The whole way to the bus stop I did not speak a word. Just dug
the heels of my boots into the gravel. Basking in the beast
of my anger.

ANYWAY

I wait for joy. It comes.
It goes. I create joy.

It comes. It goes.
I seek joy. It comes.

It goes. I smile, and
the world tells me

not to. I smile anyway.

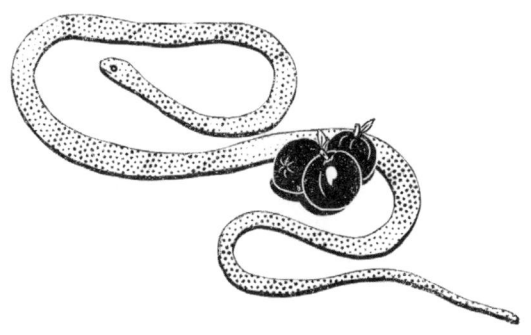

IV

QUESTIONS MY DAUGHTER ASKS

Do animals have calendars?
Is an avocado a fruit or a vegetable?
If it's spring, does that mean
I can wear skirts everyday?

Can I pretend this is a scooter?
Can I pretend this is a pony?
Can you just say whatever you want
when you think of it?

How do you design an acorn?
How did you get those lines *there
on that plush tissue of stomach,
raised garden beds,
peach blistered over?*

Do you feel them *like whistling silver-white
spider web*s when you inhale?

Will I get them too, when I am a woman?
Why does life leave so much evidence behind?

THE BRA

You know the one/ shuffled from bag
to drawer to carry on/ felt by different
hands/ seen by different eyes/ burnt
by the flat iron/ settles over your chest
like a prophecy/ remember when Ashley
tried to steal it that night/ after the
dancing/ after the moon had tucked itself
into the sky's violet pocket/ with sweat still
pooled in the lining/ *just makes the girls pop*,
she said/ thick straps paired with sturdy
catches/ after so many years/ and for
most of them/ the only consistency.

SUCCESS

This week, not one low balance
alert from the bank. Hidden in my

desk drawer is a love letter to dandelions,
the same burnt yellow of a slow simmer

curry. I finally recognize myself
in our shared resilience. After

work, you kiss me full on the mouth.
The children are playing.

INTERSECTION OF WAR AND GOOD INTENTIONS

The world continues to destroy
like water, least resistance.

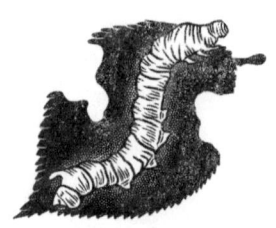

FOR CLARIFICATION

Flesh is not particularly interesting,
nor complicated. It isn't clever on its own,

although it can be. It doesn't understand
comedic timing. It isn't especially gifted

with a metaphor. When it is cold out, it gets cold.
When I smile, I crinkle like decadent French pastry.

I stand at the stove in slippers on Sundays. Eggs
cracked and simmering into breakfast eligibility. A body,

eager for sustenance. A woman, tired. A mother,
listening to the rising decibel of weekend morning

chaos. Again and again, I raise a fork to my lips
like a smug red flag whipping towards a bull.
Again and again, every fluffy bite is eaten.

SCIENTIFIC STUDIES SUGGEST MENTAL HEALTH IS BETTER WHEN THERE ARE MORE WINDOWS IN ANY GIVEN ROOM

We want so little and we ask for even less. A window, a room, a town, a city, a country, a place to safely call our own. A place

of existential continuation, as phoenix tuft and feather, that claims us with equal fervor. Do you believe in aliens? Or at the very least, breath

in a different shape, as a different sort of creature. Mammal or reptilian, or an altogether unobserved mass of cells and intellect.

I read recently that outsider space crafts have already made contact. The author of the article did not seem the least bit surprised. In truth,

there is no record of mass hysteria. No clamor of unrest.
Surely, we aim to co-exist. We want life, just the same. We
do. We only wish for

boredom. Slower speeds. No news. Cozy, static airwaves. At
minimum, less juxtaposition. There are planets circulating,
ebbing like Viking battle

grounds, yet we narrow ours to thimbles. What to wear,
who to love, how to fit. In any life form we would want
those basic, animal comforts. All of

us small, soft padded mice nibbling through winter walls to
find some measure of shelter. All of us waiting on the other
end of the phone for

someone we love, somewhere, to let us know they made it
home alright.

OF COURSE, TAKE THE UMBRELLA

Grab the coat, too. Pack the extra snack. Be prepared for the unexpected.
Better yet, create the unexpected wherever you can. By whatever means necessary.

Buy a dozen oranges and eat them until you are absolutely full of citrus.
Take off your shoes in the long, cool grass and thread your toes into the blades.

Wash up green with happiness. Lather on sunscreen and bury yourself in the sand. Stand on the top of a mountain and scream into the sky. Do the same from your open apartment window.

Drink your coffee black, just once, just to try it. Put away all of your distractions.
Make new ones. Big, messy ones. Climb a tree, and at the top, whisper to the leaves about all of your worries. When you climb back down, let them stay there.

Wherever you are going, take the back road. Write a ten-page letter about nothing but the weather and your admiration for Sunday dinners. Mail it to someone you love.

Read philosophy and fiction with tight storylines. Once a week, wash your sheets and climb into them immediately steaming and hot from the dryer. Stay there all afternoon.

Try every food on the menu at your favorite restaurant. Recite a poem until you find it out of habit. Cross as many state lines as you can in one day.

Follow all of the instructions, or don't. Maybe try writing your own. Your story has not been decided yet. It won't be until the very end.

Question everything. Sometimes it is okay to forget the deadlines.

Laugh as much as you can, at yourself, at the world around you. At the beauty that is happening all of the time, in each impossible moment.

Remember all of the gray space between right and wrong. Try to be as gentle with yourself as you can. If you need help, ask for it. If someone else needs help, offer it.

There isn't an instruction manual for anything worthwhile. But I promise, you will never regret being present. This life is a passing glance, a momentary blip of rotation.
It cannot stay; it isn't meant to. Open yourself to joy.
Please, I insist.

Alison Malee is a poet, artist, author, and performer. Her poetry collections *Shifting Bone, The Day Is Ready For You, This Is The Journey,* and *It Is All Equally Fragile,* are about expression, family, femininity, and the possibility that exists within us.

instagram.com/alison.malee
facebook.com/alisonamalee

THOUGHT CATALOG Books

Thought Catalog Books is a publishing imprint of Thought Catalog, a digital magazine for thoughtful storytelling, and is owned and operated by The Thought & Expression Co. Inc., an independent media group based in the United States of America. Founded in 2010, we are committed to helping people become better communicators and listeners to engender a more exciting, attentive, and imaginative world. The Thought Catalog Books imprint connects Thought Catalog's digital-native roots with our love of traditional book publishing. The books we publish are designed as beloved art pieces. We publish work we love. Pioneering an author-first and holistic approach to book publishing, Thought Catalog Books has created numerous best-selling print books, audiobooks, and eBooks that are being translated in over 30 languages.

ThoughtCatalog.com | **Thoughtful Storytelling**

ShopCatalog.com | **Shop Books + Curated Products**

**MORE FROM
THOUGHT CATALOG BOOKS**

Moments To Hold Close
—*Molly Burford*

When You're Ready, This Is How You Heal
—*Brianna Wiest*

The Unbearable Beauty
—*Annabelle Blythe*

Holding Space for the Sun
—*Jamal Cadoura*

All The Right Pieces
—*Nakeia Homer*

How to Laugh in Ironic Amusement
During Your Existential Crisis
—*James McCrae*

THOUGHT CATALOG Books

THOUGHTCATALOG.COM